EXPLORE
ANCIENT
WORLDS

ANCIENT
BABYLON

Karen Bush Gibson

Mitchell Lane
PUBLISHERS

P.O. Box 196
Hockessin, Delaware 19707
Visit us on the web: www.mitchelllane.com
Comments? email us: contactus@mitchelllane.com

EXPLORE ANCIENT WORLDS

Ancient Assyria • Ancient Athens
The Aztecs • Ancient Babylon
The Byzantine Empire • The Celts of the British Isles
Ancient China • Ancient Egypt
Ancient India/Maurya Empire • Ancient Sparta

Copyright © 2013 by Mitchell Lane Publishers

Printing 1 2 3 4 5 6 7 8 9

ABOUT THE AUTHOR: Karen Bush Gibson enjoys learning about other cultures. She has written dozens of books about cultures, history, and other subjects for children. She is also the author of The Amazon and Railroads Come to America for Mitchell Lane Publishers.

PUBLISHER'S NOTE: The facts on which the story in this book is based have been thoroughly researched. Documentation of such research can be found on page 45. While every possible effort has been made to ensure accuracy, the publisher will not assume liability for damages caused by inaccuracies in the data, and makes no warranty on the accuracy of the information contained herein.

Library of Congress
Cataloging-in-Publication Data
Gibson, Karen Bush.
 Ancient Babylon / by Karen Gibson.
   p. cm. — (Explore ancient worlds)
 Includes bibliographical references and index.
 ISBN 978-1-61228-278-7 (library bound)
 1. Babylonia—Juvenile literature. I. Title.
 DS71.G53 2012
 935'.5—dc23
                                    2012008636

eBook ISBN: 9781612283531

                                    PLB

CONTENTS

The Tower of Babel

CHAPTER 1

Babylon: A Wonder of the Ancient World

Arshaka stood on the hill and looked down on the huge city of Babylon. He had come from Assur, a smaller city located north of Babylon. A carpenter by trade, he came to Babylon to visit his sister, Amata. She had just given birth to her first child.

Arshaka had never seen anything like Babylon. Tall walls surrounded the entire city. Canals and streets criss-crossed each other, creating many squares. Each square was filled with buildings or crops. The midday sun reflected off the tallest buildings. Hundreds of people went about their business in the streets.

The traveler climbed down from the hill to the Processional Way, the main street into the city. It was paved with white limestone bordered by red granite, which was marbled with thin white lines. Arshaka looked closer at the writing on the granite stones. They were engraved with the name Nebuchadnezzar, one of Babylon's famous kings.

On Arshaka's right was the Northern Palace. This was the newer palace, sometimes called the Summer Palace. King Nebuchadnezzar used vertical ventilation shafts to cool it.

Enormous animal statues seemed to look down on Arshaka as he approached the monumental Ishtar Gate. One of eight gates into the city, it was the main entrance and stood nearly 39 feet (12 meters) high. The

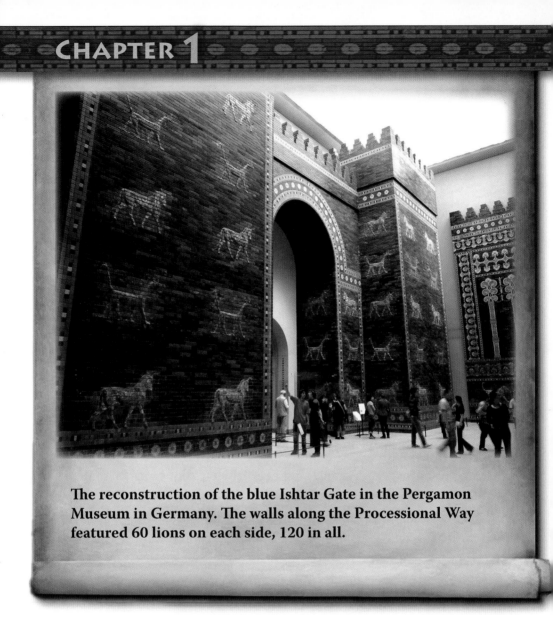

The reconstruction of the blue Ishtar Gate in the Pergamon Museum in Germany. The walls along the Processional Way featured 60 lions on each side, 120 in all.

brilliant blue glazed brick gate was decorated with pictures of 150 bulls and dragons.[1]

Arshaka looked at the carved lions that adorned the walls. There were 120 of them. Some were yellow with red manes. Others were white with yellow manes. They were symbols of the goddess Ishtar, for whom the gate was named.

Ishtar, the goddess of love and fertility, was the most famous goddess of Babylon. In mythology, she would be compared to the Greek goddess

Aphrodite. Ishtar was the daughter of Anu, the god of air. Many myths showed her as an evil woman who destroyed her mates.

Arshaka passed through the gate, entering the older part of the city where a market was being held. People buying and selling fresh fruits and vegetables, wool, and other goods surrounded him. The sweet aroma of pastries made his mouth water. He bought wine, bread, and cheese for his next meal.

He wanted a gift for his wife, Iltani. When he touched a necklace, the jeweler gave a price. Arshaka shook his head. It was too much. The seller didn't give up. They haggled over the price until reaching an amount both agreed on.

After looking at a warm coat for himself, Arshaka continued along the Processional Way. Soon he passed the Southern Palace. Many rooms surrounded five courtyards of this older, main palace. Servants and guards lived near the first courtyard. Administrative staff lived around the second courtyard. The third courtyard was next to the throne room. The king's private quarters surrounded the fourth courtyard. The fifth courtyard was for the king's harem.

Although the Southern Palace was impressive, Arshaka had come a long way to see something else—the ziggurat, or great tower. Standing nearly 300 feet (90 meters) high, it was the city's tallest structure. The Babylonians called it Etemenanki, meaning "house of the foundation of heaven on earth."[2] The square building looked like a tower of blocks, with each level smaller than the one below it.

A ziggurat was a type of temple dedicated to a god. In Babylon, that god was Marduk. The Greek historian Herodotus, who wrote a detailed description of Babylon and its history, called Marduk the Babylonian version of the supreme Greek god, Zeus.

Many historians believe that Babylon's ziggurat was the Tower of Babel mentioned in the Bible's Book of Genesis. This story states that everyone in the world once spoke the same language. They built the Tower of Babel, hoping to reach the heavens. This effort angered God. Punishing them for their conceit and ambition, God made them speak different languages so that they couldn't understand one another. This is the origin of the word *babble,* meaning "to talk in confusion."

Whether it was the Tower of Babel or not, the ziggurat's blue enamel bricks shone brightly in the Babylonian sun. Now that he was closer, the traveler could make out some of the various plants and flowers on its terraces.

Time and war had taken a toll on the ziggurat. It had to be rebuilt many times. Each time, it became a little higher. There have been many guesses about how many floors it actually contained. Herodotus described the tower: "It has a solid central tower, one stadium square, with a second erected on top of it and then a third, and so on up to eight."[3]

Poet and artist William Blake painted Nebuchadnezzar II as a man, then suffering from insanity after his rule over Babylon.

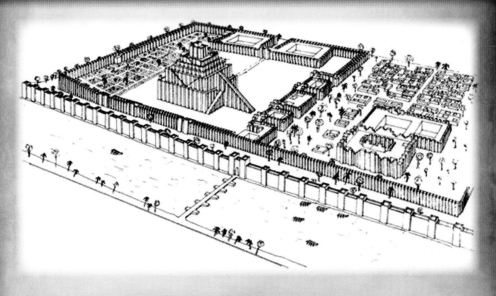

The Temple of Marduk was considered one of the most important buildings in Babylon.

A height of eight stories was impressive during a time when most Babylonian buildings were two or three stories. The tower was also far larger than the neighboring Temple of Marduk, known as the Temple of Belus to the Greeks and Esagila to the Babylonians (*Esagila* is Sumerian for "the house that raises its head."[4]).

Even though it wasn't the largest building in Babylon, the Temple of Marduk was important. It was a complex built around two courtyards. Arshaka entered the first of the two courtyards, an area 230 feet long and 131 feet wide (70 meters by 40 meters).

A priest allowed Arshaka to come inside the smaller, but more important courtyard. It was the same width, but less than half as long at 82 feet (25 meters). This courtyard led to two rooms: an anteroom and the room that contained the shrine. The inner walls, covered in sparkling gold, shone like the sun. Even more wondrous was the statue of Marduk which Herodotus said was made from 22 tons of gold and stood 15 feet high. After Arshaka gave thanks to Marduk for a safe journey, he continued exploring the city.

The Euphrates River separated the old and new sections of the city of Babylon.

He came to the Euphrates Bridge. As he stood in the middle, he could see how the Euphrates River divided the city between the old and the new. Approximately 660 yards (600 meters) long, the bridge included artistic details like what he had seen at the gate and the temples.

Arshaka saw other temples as well: the Temple of Ishtar of Agade, the Temple of Gula, the Temple of Adad, the Temple of Shamash, and others. During Babylon's history, it is estimated that nearly 1,200 temples were built and dedicated to both major and minor gods.

Another wondrous thing was the Hanging Gardens of Babylon. It was a park within the city regarded as one of the Seven Wonders of the Ancient World.

The ability to build such an amazing city was evidence of the knowledge of the Babylonians. In most cases, they applied their knowledge to everyday life. When he returned home, Arshaka had much to share about the amazing city of Babylon.

The Seven Wonders of the Ancient World

The Hanging Gardens

Much like people today, people of ancient civilizations were list makers. One of the most famous lists, the Seven Wonders of the World, was compiled by the Greek poet Antipater of Sidon in about 140 BCE. Antipater listed what he thought were the seven greatest sights in his world. Not surprisingly, four of them were connected with Greece: the statue of Zeus in Olympia and the giant statue of the sun god Helios known as the Colossus of Rhodes were in Greece itself, while the Temple of Artemis in Ephesus and the world's first mausoleum at Halicarnassus had been constructed by Greek settlers in what is modern-day Turkey.

The Great Pyramid of Egypt was another of the world's wonders. The 450-foot (137-meter) high pyramid was built as a tomb for the Pharaoh Khufu. Until the fourteenth century CE, it was the world's tallest building.

The remaining two wonders were in Babylon: the Hanging Gardens and the immense walls that surrounded the city. Eventually the Alexandria lighthouse in Egypt would replace the Babylonian walls on other lists. Of the Seven Wonders of the Ancient World, only the Hanging Gardens have never been proven to exist. Some people believe these gardens are a legend. Others think that perhaps the Hanging Gardens and the Garden of Eden were the same.

Today, only the Great Pyramid of Egypt still exists. Some of the wonders have disappeared entirely. Of the other sites, only ruins remain.

Many people thought Babylon was an imaginary place until nineteenth-century archaeologists began to uncover parts of the city.

CHAPTER 2

When History Began

One of the earliest human civilizations arose in Sumer, an area between the Persian Gulf and eastern shore of the Mediterranean Sea, more than 6,500 years ago. The inhabitants were called Sumerians. Sumer and the land surrounding it eventually became known as Mesopotamia, or "land between the rivers." Mesopotamia lay between two main rivers, the Tigris and the Euphrates. Both rivers flowed from the mountains of what is today southeastern Turkey to the Persian Gulf. The land was divided into a series of city-states. City-states were made up of a city and its surrounding villages. Babylonia was one of Mesopotamia's city-states, and its capital was Babylon, a Greek name meaning "gate of god."

More than 2,500 years ago, the Persians conquered Mesopotamia. Now the land is covered by Iraq and parts of Iran, Syria, and Turkey.

Much of what we know about ancient Babylon comes from two sources. One is the Bible, which states that the mighty hunter Nimrod was the founder of Babylon. The Bible refers to Babylon as a city of great power, wealth, and godlessness.

The other source of information about Babylon comes from documents in cuneiform writing, the earliest known form of writing. Textbooks, novels, and business contracts written in cuneiform have been found. These and other records tell of a city called Babylon, whose first mention comes from about 2300 BCE.

It was founded as a small farming village, located in the "Fertile Crescent." This was a stretch of territory that extended from Mesopotamia west and south to the Nile River Valley in Egypt. It is nicknamed the "Cradle of Civilization" because so many ancient civilizations arose there, due to its excellent soil for growing crops and warm climate.

The soil in Babylon came from the sediment of the rivers. Many crops thrived in the fertile ground, including fruit such as pomegranates and dates, grains such as wheat, and vegetables such as onions, garlic, leeks, turnips, cucumbers, and lettuce. The most important crop was barley—the staple of Babylonian society. It was used for making both bread and beer. Where the water didn't reach naturally, people dug canals to irrigate their fields. Farmers used oxen to pull wagons and seeder-plows. A Mesopotamian invention, the seeder-plow simultaneously plowed and planted the fields with seeds.

The pastures fed herds of goats, sheep, pigs, and cattle. The animals provided meat and milk, which was used to make yogurt and cheese. Milk was also the base for some medicines.

People of Babylon usually ate two meals a day, in the morning and evening. The wealthy ate better—meat, bread, and beer, often with pastries and fatty foods. Fish was important to early Babylonian diets, but not later. No one knows why.

The two rivers made many things possible. They provided water to people, animals, and crops. Farmers lived in sturdy houses made from river mud. The rivers also connected communities. Babylonians made woven rugs and traded them for things like teakwood and cotton from India. Heavy items were carried down the rivers on rafts made of inflated animal skins. People also traveled on lightweight boats, known as coracles, which were made of wicker and covered in animal skins.

Peaceful times were rare in early Babylon. Leaders of other regions also wanted to expand their kingdoms. The Sumerians and Babylonians were sometimes overpowered by other groups—Assyrians, Semites, Elamites, and Amorites.

This photograph, taken in 1932, shows how narrow the streets of Babylon could be.

Still, Babylon grew into a major cultural center under the direction of successful leaders. Streets were laid out like many city streets of today—straight lines that intersected with other straight lines. Some of the streets were quite narrow, not much wider than a sidewalk. Others were as much as 20 feet (6 meters) wide, about the same size as a modern two-lane road. Except for the Processional Way, Babylon's streets consisted of dirt.

People used the streets to get from their homes to public buildings and temples. They also used the streets as a garbage dump. Like other cities in early history, Babylonians threw their garbage out their windows and onto the streets. When the garbage piled high enough, they covered the streets with clay. When these layers of garbage and clay grew too high, people had to build steps down to their front doors or rebuild their houses on higher ground.

As Babylon grew, so did its industries. In addition to farmers and shepherds, there were carpenters, wine makers, potters, surveyors, and weavers. Many craftsmen worked on leather or metal, dyed cloth, or made bricks.

Brickmaking became a very important industry because it was hard to find stone or wood. There was even a month in late spring dedicated to

A Babylonian model of a sheep's liver, with writings of omens and magic formulas.

making bricks. Babylonian bricks were made from mud and dried in the sun or baked in an oven. For each building, a foundation of rectangular bricks was laid. Like today's homes and buildings, foundations provided more stability.

Physicians were part of Babylonian society too. They healed people with a combination of magic and medicine. Many diseases were believed to be caused by demons in the body. Although an ancient text mentions a female physician, almost all physicians were male. The exception were midwives, women who helped with childbirth.

Babylon had three main social classes: free men (which included the king and nobles), free laborers and slaves. Captives from war or foreigners from other countries became slaves to work in the fields or in manufacturing. Temple slaves waited on kings and priests. Babylonian slaves were treated better than slaves in other societies. Children were not separated from parents. Often, slaves could buy their freedom. Free laborers often did the same type of work as slaves. However, free laborers had a written contract of work with an employer. They also had the choice of hiring themselves out to work for others.

Babylon was a male-dominated society. Men made most of the decisions, and the father was the head of the household. Sometimes this power was transferred to the mother upon her husband's death. Grooms often paid brides' fathers to be able to marry their daughters. However, many wives also came to marriage with a dowry. Husbands could have more than one wife. A husband could also divorce a wife as long as he let her take the dowry she had brought to the marriage.

In Babylon, if a son argued with his parents, he could be disowned. If that happened, he no longer would be part of the family.

The First Writing

Cuneiform writing was the world's first writing system. It originated about 5,500 years ago, and consisted of several hundred basic wedge-shaped signs. More symbols were developed over time and in different city-states. The person who

Cuneiform writing

did the writing was called a scribe. A scribe wrote on a clay tablet with a wooden or reed stylus.

Learning how to do cuneiform writing was only for a chosen few, and they came from wealthy families. Nearly all of them were boys, who were chosen at a young age to attend a special school called a tablet house, which taught its students how to be scribes. Students attended school from sunrise to sunset for up to twelve years. They learned cuneiform writing by memorizing word lists and copying from textbooks and documents. They also learned science, mathematics, and grammar.

After graduating, a scribe might work in government or as an assistant to important people. Scribes were hired both to write letters and to read them. Early writing was used for business contracts and making lists, but it soon expanded. Omens, thought to be communications from the gods, were written down. Astronomy, mathematics, medicine, and science all appeared in cuneiform documents. "Wisdom literature" included fables, philosophical works, and epics. *The Epic of Creation* and *The Epic of Gilgamesh* were the two most important epics.

Babylonians were fascinated by the stars and used them to make predictions about omens that would occur. They also made the signs of the Zodiac, such as Sagittarius the Archer.

Gods and Kings

Religion was at the center of Babylonian life. Babylonians believed that the Earth was an upside-down bowl. People lived on the surface of the bowl; within the bowl were the dead. Above the bowl were the heavens where many gods lived—beyond the moon, stars, and sun.

Through religion, Babylonians created scientific and mathematical knowledge still in use today. Ancient Babylonians used astrology—the knowledge of how the planets and stars move—to predict omens. For example, if the moon and sun were seen together six days within a month, it meant a war was coming. Around 400 BCE, they began writing horoscopes based on the signs of the zodiac.

Babylonians needed to measure time, length, capacity, and area, so they created units of measurement. Corn was the basis of weight at first, but later silver became the standard. Early texts show that educated people could perform many different mathematical functions. One flaw in Babylonian math was that there doesn't appear to be a symbol for zero.

Babylonians invented the sundial to tell time. Time was divided into twelve units between sunrise and sunset.

The Babylonians also used the sundial to tell time. Today's timekeeping system of using 60 seconds to equal a minute and 60 minutes to equal an hour began in Babylon, though there's no way of telling how they measured such short time intervals.

The Babylonian year of 354 days started in the spring. Each of the twelve months lasted for one lunar cycle, from one New Moon phase to the next, either 29 or 30 days. Because the solar year is 365 and 1/4 days, the seasons of the year slowly drifted from month to month. To correct this, Babylonian kings occasionally added a leap month on the advice of astronomers.

In the religion of Mesopotamia, each city was dedicated to one of the gods. For Babylon, that god was Marduk, who created the earth and heavens. Marduk was a god born from the freshwater sea. Tiamat was a huge dragon that represented the ocean, also called "chaos water." Marduk protected the other gods by killing Tiamat. Killing the monster led to order (the opposite of chaos) in the universe.

The name "Marduk" was rarely used in conversation because people thought it was too holy to be said out loud. Instead, Babylonians used the word Bel, which meant "Lord." Marduk was the supreme god or leader of the gods. This made Babylon a very important city in ancient Mesopotamia.

Religious life and festivals of Babylon revolved around temples. The most important was the Temple of Marduk. It was the center of the universe.

An altar was placed outside the temple. There, people gave frankincense to the god during the New Year's Festival, the most important festival in Babylon. During this festival, the other gods (represented by their statues) left their cities to visit Marduk and declare their plans for the next year.

The New Year's Festival, called the Akitu Festival, was held around March or April. This was the time that barley could be planted. Festivities lasted for a week at Marduk's temple and at the New Year house in the northern part of the city. The celebration spilled out onto the Processional Way, which connected the two locations. The festival was filled with rituals that started with a priest reciting *The Epic of Creation.* The people celebrated with songs and feasts.

Every Babylonian's purpose in life was to serve the gods. Each household prayed and gave sacrifices to a personal god. Priests ran the temples. Their job was to drive away evil spirits and help the king. The early kings of Babylon served as representatives of the gods, providing the gods with temples and wealth. Many rulers also placed a statue of themselves in the temple to be looked on favorably by the gods. In this way, kings were also worshipped.

The king was a warrior too. The most successful kings defended their people and conquered other city-states. The Babylonian king was like the president, the legislature, and the court system all rolled up into one. He directed a group of governors to help run the kingdom. City councils of respected elders made the minor decisions. There was even a type of post office to deliver letters in Babylonia.

One of many lists written by Babylonian scribes was the Great List of Kings. It covers over a thousand years and mentions nine Babylonian dynasties, the names of approximately seventy kings, and the years they ruled. Although parts of the list are missing, it helps show the different time periods of ancient Babylon.

The first dynasty, sometimes referred to as the Old Babylon period, began about 1895 BCE. Its founder was Sumu-Abum, the first of 11 kings during this period. During his reign, the palace was built. Temples, such as the Ishtar Temple, first appeared. He also began construction of the walls.

The most famous of the first dynasty of Babylonian kings was Hammurabi, who was the sixth. After coming to power in 1792 BCE, King Hammurabi declared Babylon the capital of Mesopotamia and ruled for 42 years.

The capital city grew under Hammurabi's rule to become a center of trade and culture. The king was also greatly concerned about justice for all Babylonians. So he created laws for people to follow—the Code of Hammurabi. Although Hammurabi died about 1750 BCE, his influence remained.

Babylon eventually fell under the control of other countries for more than a thousand years. However, the city's reputation as a cultural center lived on. Starting about 1600 BCE, the Kassite kings ruled Babylon for more than 600 years. Despite the length of their rule, modern archaeologists and historians know little about them.

Assyria then overpowered the Kassite kings for control of Babylon. A good deal of Hammurabi's Babylon was destroyed. An Assyrian king banished the people of Babylon from their city. He stated that Babylon was to be in ruins for 70 years. Yet after 11 years, Assyrian King Esarhaddon allowed the Babylonians to return.

Babylon's last and greatest dynasty, the Neo-Babylonian dynasty, began in 626 BCE when a Babylonian general named Nabopolassar led a successful revolt against the Assyrians. Once again, Babylon became one of the most important cities among ancient civilizations. Much of the importance of Babylon was due to King Nabopolassar's son, Nebuchadnezzar II.

Nebuchadnezzar II had served as the head of his father's military. He inherited the throne when Nabopolassar died in 605 BCE. Nebuchadnezzar

King Nebuchadnezzar captured Jerusalem and destroyed much of it before sending the people to Babylon as slaves.

II used his knowledge to conquer other countries and bring their treasures to Babylon.

King Nebuchadnezzar led his armies to conquer Syria and Egypt. During the long struggle with Egypt, he captured Jerusalem, a city of Judea and the center of the Hebrew, or Jewish, religion. He forced many thousands of Jewish people to serve as slaves in Babylon.

Babylon grew under King Nebuchadnezzar's watchful eye. His success with conquests and control of trade routes led to building and rebuilding Babylon. To protect the city, he had two thick brick walls built around it. While Herodotus said that the walls measured 60 miles (96 kilometers) all the way around, they were actually quite a bit less, perhaps 11 or 12 miles (18 kilometers). They may have been as high as 80 feet (25 meters).

Reportedly, King Nebuchadnezzar created the Hanging Gardens of Babylon for his wife. She was homesick for the meadows and mountains of her home. He used colored and scented plants from all over the known world. The air around the gardens must have been perfumed with plants like citrus trees and rose bushes.

The gardens were like a park with flowers, shrubs, and trees. According to Greek historian Diodorus Siculus, the Hanging Gardens were about 400

No one knows what the Hanging Gardens of Babylon looked like, but many have created paintings and models like this of what they imagine it looked like.

feet (121 meters) on each side. They may have been located on a rooftop or perhaps on the terraces 80 feet (25 meters) above the ground.[1] Vines spilling over from the terraces or a rooftop would create a garden that looked like it was hanging. Trees and other plants grew from planters of baked brick bonded in cement. Slaves worked devices called water engines to take water from the Euphrates River for the garden.

The time of the great Babylonian kings ended with Nebuchadnezzar's death in 562 BCE, after 43 years of rule. His son, Amel-Marduk, succeeded him, but only ruled two years before he was murdered. Amel-Marduk's sister, Kassaya, had married Neriglissar. It is possible that Neriglissar had something to do with Amel-Marduk's death. Neriglissar died after ruling for three years. His son took control of the Babylonian throne, but was overthrown by a powerful Babylonian nobleman. The nobleman had his father placed on the throne. The new king was Nabonidus, and he would be the last king of an independent Babylon.

Hammurabi's Code of Laws

King Hammurabi believed that everyone, no matter who they were, should follow certain rules. Many of these laws had been around for years, but Hammurabi brought them all together and put them in writing on a black slab of stone, known as the stele of Hammurabi.

Hammurabi

Hammurabi's Code included 282 laws. Just like the U.S. Constitution, the Code began with a preamble. It stated that the gods gave Hammurabi the power to "rule of righteousness in the land, to destroy the wicked and the evil-doers; so that the strong should not harm the weak; so that I should rule over the black-headed people like Shamash, and enlighten the land, to further the well-being of mankind."[2]

The Code had laws about family, including marriage, divorce, adoption, and inheritance. There were also laws about crimes against others, such as stealing. Many laws were about business, including business contracts, loans, and partnerships. Babylonian justice was often based on the idea of "an eye for an eye." The code stated that physicians should be paid according to the patient's social status. But if the physician made any mistakes during surgery, he could be punished with mutilation or death. If a builder built a house that collapsed on an owner, the builder would be put to death. A son who hit his father would have his hand cut off.

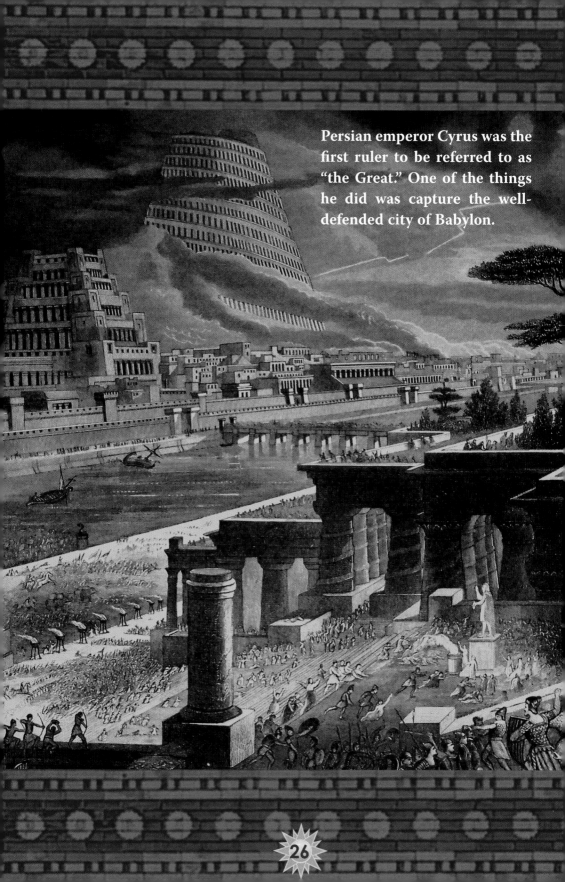

Persian emperor Cyrus was the first ruler to be referred to as "the Great." One of the things he did was capture the well-defended city of Babylon.

CHAPTER 4

The Fall of Babylon

King Nabonidus assumed the Babylonian throne in 556 BCE. One of his main concerns was making the Babylonian empire even bigger. One way was by controlling the trade routes. In 553 BCE, he invaded Arabia, which lay to the west. He left the crown prince and other officials in charge of Babylon while he was gone.

Nabonidus returned to his kingdom in 543 BCE, perhaps realizing that a major threat to his capital city came from the east. Cyrus, the king of Persia, or modern-day Iran, had already conquered several nearby kingdoms and city-states. The first ruler to be referred to as "the Great," Cyrus founded the Achaemenid Empire, the largest empire the world had yet known. It would last more than 200 years.

Nabonidus' reign was weakened because he angered many priests in Babylon. He wanted to replace Marduk as the most important god with Sin, who had been important to the Assyrians.

In October 539 BCE, Cyrus and his forces captured Opis, a city on the east bank of the Tigris River. It was also on the Royal Road, a trade route that linked important cities throughout Mesopotamia and Assyria.

Cyrus and his troops set out for Babylon. The Persian army reached the city quickly from a nearby canal that linked the Tigris and Euphrates

Rivers. In addition to speeding up travel between the two rivers, the canal created a moat to protect Babylon.

The people of Babylon had suspected that the Persians might attack. The Babylonians stocked everything they would need for a long siege and settled behind the walls of their city. Nothing could break through them. According to Herodotus, the walls were so thick—87 feet (26 meters)—that a four-horse chariot could easily turn around on top of them.

Cyrus left part of his army where the Euphrates River enters Babylon. His remaining forces dug a basin in a nearby marsh. As the river rushed in to fill the basin, the water level at the entrance to the city dropped drastically.

When the river was only thigh-high, Cyrus and his army waded through it and into the city. Most of the Babylonians didn't know that the Persian army had arrived. They were miles away in the center of the city at a festival. Cyrus had the element of surprise on his side and captured Babylon without much trouble.

Cyrus entering Babylon

Much of what we know about the fall of Babylon came from the Cyrus Cylinder, discovered by archaeologists in the nineteenth century.

In 1879 CE, archaeologists recovered a clay cylinder. It was called the Cyrus Cylinder because it gives the Persian ruler's version of the fall of Babylon. Today it sits in the British Museum. According to the cylinder, Cyrus was successful because Marduk, the god of Babylon, had announced Cyrus "aloud for the kingship over all."[1]

Cyrus claimed to be "king of the universe, the great king, the powerful king, king of Babylon, king of Sumer and Akkad, king of the four quarters of the world."[2] And indeed his accomplishments were many. Cyrus returned statues of gods stolen by Nabonidus to their original shrines in other Mesopotamian cities. He also added to Babylon's walls with stronger gates made of cedar and copper.

Cyrus' written decree from the cylinder has been described by some people as the first declaration of human rights in history. He supported religious and cultural freedom for all and also brought an end to slavery. He saw himself not as a conqueror, but as a liberator who "shepherded in justice and righteousness all the black-headed people."[3] This statement most likely referred to people of all nations, but particularly to the Jewish people who had been removed from their homes by King Nebuchadnezzar II several decades earlier. The Jewish slaves in Babylon cheered when Cyrus conquered the city. One of his actions was to release Babylonian captives so they could return to their homelands. This included thousands of Jews.

According to author H.G. Wells in his book *A Short History of the World,* the Jewish captives returned home with all the knowledge they had gained in Babylon. They created a large body of literature, including laws, poetry, books of wisdom, and fiction. They also recorded their history in the Torah, the first five books of the Old Testament of the Bible.

Babylon never regained the splendor it once had. Although it continued as a religious and scientific center for several centuries, it took on qualities from the cultures that conquered it. For example, the Southern Palace, which was the main palace, had columns typically seen in Persian buildings. This addition may have been made by Darius, the Persian ruler who had to reconquer Babylon when the city revolted after the death of Cyrus the Great. Because it took Darius twenty months to successfully gain control of Babylon, he destroyed all the city gates. The Babylonians would never be able to lock anyone out of their city again.

More than 200 years later, in 331 BCE, another "Great" leader took over Babylon. That was Alexander the Great, who planned to restore Babylon and make it the center of his world empire. When Alexander arrived in Babylon, the public buildings had been neglected and had suffered damage during battles. One of the first things he planned to do was rebuild the Tower of Babel. Debris had already been moved away to prepare for rebuilding. But when Alexander died suddenly in 323 BCE, his plans to return Babylon to its former glory were never followed.

Alexander the Great

Alexander the Great

Alexander enters Babylon

Alexander the Great was born in 356 BCE in Macedonia, a kingdom at the northeastern edge of Greece. His father, King Philip II, had already turned Macedonia into a powerful nation. When Alexander turned thirteen, his tutor—the noted Greek philosopher Aristotle—taught him literature, philosophy, oratory, science, and medicine.

When Alexander turned sixteen, his father left him in charge of Macedonia while he led his armies against another country. Two years later, Alexander was made a senior general of the Macedonian army.

After the assassination of his father in 336 BCE, Alexander became king of Macedonia. Some countries rebelled against the new young leader. Demonstrating superior military strategy, Alexander conquered Greece, Thrace, and Illyria before setting out in 334 to conquer the Persian Empire, as his father had intended. He was only twenty-two years old.

Alexander's army met the Persians at the Granicus River. Alexander's forces defeated the Persian army, losing only about 300 men to 4,000 Persians. For the next 10 years, Alexander continued his advance through the Middle East, winning battle after battle. He penetrated as far as India before being forced to retreat.

While in Babylon in 323 BCE, Alexander suddenly became ill and died. He was only thirty-three years old, and the cause of his death has always been a mystery. Was it poison? An illness? Without its leader, the Macedonian empire began to fall apart. About a century and a half later, the Romans conquered Macedonia and it became part of the Roman Empire.

Alexander the Great captured Babylon, but died a mysterious death soon after in this depiction by German painter Karl von Piloty.

Today's Babylon

When Alexander the Great died, several of his most important generals divided up his empire. One of them was Seleucus, who took over Babylon in 312 BCE. Seven years later, he built a new city called Seleucia on the Tigris River. Many people from Babylon were ordered to move there. The population continued to decline. By the time the Roman emperor Trajan visited the site in 116–117 CE, the city was little more than ruins.

Starting in the 1800s, Europeans and Americans became interested in the history of the Middle East. Places mentioned in Greek, Roman, and biblical writings were especially popular. One of the first European explorers was a young Englishman named Claudius James Rich, who began working for the East India Company in Baghdad in 1813. Having a strong interest in ancient ruins, he visited the site where Babylon had been located. He made a map of what remained of the ancient city.

For several centuries, visitors to Babylonian and Mesopotamian ruins noticed the cuneiform tablets, but no one knew what they meant. They were like a secret code until several scholars, most notably a British archaeologist named Henry Rawlinson, began deciphering some of the tablets starting about 1835. Rawlinson eventually published several books detailing the results of his research.

British and French archaeologists began excavating various Mesopotamian sites at the end of the nineteenth century. They found pottery, which helped them build a timeline of the civilizations that had lived there.

When World War I ended in 1918, much of Mesopotamia and all of Babylonia came under British control. The British named the territory Iraq, an Arabic term that had been in wide use since the region became part of the Islamic empire in about 640 CE. The British established a monarchy in 1921, and the Kingdom of Iraq became independent 11 years later. Iraq became a republic in 1958 when the kingdom was overthrown. For a long time, the remains of crumbling mud brick buildings offered visitors a glimpse into the past. It is believed that people used the bricks from Babylon to build new temples and homes in the nearby city of Hilla.

In 1987, Iraqi leader Saddam Hussein decided he wanted to rebuild one of the palaces from the rubble. He had a palace built like he thought King Nebuchadnezzar might have had on a hill overlooking the ancient ruins.

Iraqi leader Saddam Hussein built a modern-day palace that looked over the Babylonian ruins.

The Iraqi people cheered when the statue of Saddam Hussein was pulled down.

Saddam even had his name engraved in the palace as Nebuchadnezzar had done. The $5 million price tag did not include using archaeologists to protect the artifacts at the site. Many treasures were destroyed.[1]

Although national festivals were held at the site for a few years, the palace became something of a joke after the fall of Saddam's regime in 2003. U.S. soldiers used it as a military base. War and looting have led to further destruction of Babylonian artifacts.

The capital of Iraq is Baghdad, approximately 56 miles north of ancient Babylon. A two-lane road leads to Babylon. It is hard to imagine the ancient city when soldiers are stopping traffic to inspect vehicles and their drivers. Trenches have been dug through what is left of magnificent ancient temples, and barbed wire stretches across the remaining ruins. The most obvious "artifacts" are the casings of bullets littering the ground. The modern

A helicopter flies over war-torn Iraq.

soldiers have written messages on the ancient walls. A helicopter pad sits on paved-over ruins.

Archaeologists from around the world want to know more about ancient Babylon, but the war has made it difficult. The high water table also adds to the difficulty. Old Babylon lies under the Euphrates River and is unreachable. Dams were later built across both the Euphrates and Tigris rivers, flooding areas where ruins may have been.

Backed by the new Iraqi government, the Future of Babylon is an international project organized by the World Monuments Fund. Its goal is to save Babylon for archaeological study and perhaps tourism. "Babylon represents one of the most important archaeological sites in the world," says the organization's web site. "Babylonia was a prosperous land and the remains today give scholars great insight into the sophisticated world in which Babylon was created and thrived."[2] The United States has helped with the funding. The Iraq State Board of Antiquities and Heritage is supervising the project. If the Future of Babylon project is successful, Babylon might rise again—this time as Iraq's top tourist attraction.

Babylonian Digs

We learn about history from a variety of scholars. Historians write histories from their research. Anthropologists study how humans lived in different time periods. Archaeologists provide information to both anthropologists and historians by digging up artifacts.

Robert Koldewey

Babylon was excavated between 1899 and 1917 by a German archaeologist named Robert Koldewey. His excavations, or "digs," uncovered numerous buildings and artifacts. Koldewey first used Greek and Persian resources to explain the meanings of his finds. Once the cuneiform documents could be translated, more reliable information became available.

Some of the artifacts he discovered, including the Ishtar Gate, can be seen in Germany's Pergamon Museum in Berlin. In its Babylonian Hall exhibit, visitors can see a re-creation of the Processional Way and some Babylonian buildings—including the throne room of King Nebuchadnezzar II and a model of the Tower of Babel. A copy of the Code of Hammurabi is also part of the exhibit.

The Code of Hammurabi stele is a highlight of the Near Eastern Antiquities exhibit in the famous Louvre Museum in Paris. The majority of the remaining excavated Babylonian artifacts, including over 130,000 cuneiform tablets, are owned by the British Museum in London. Experts continue to translate the cuneiform tablets.

Meanwhile, archaeologists continue to look for the site of the Hanging Gardens. Koldewey located a well in a foundation chamber that may have been part of its watering system. Perhaps the Hanging Gardens of Babylon will be discovered one day.

Babylonian Craft: Make a Sundial

What did people do before the invention of clocks and watches? They used sundials, which are based on the sun's position in the sky. The shadow the sun casts on the dial tells the time.

Note: A sundial is most accurate when it is designed for the latitude of a specific place. Latitude is the distance north or south from the equator. Various web sites or global positioning systems (GPS) give the latitude of a location. This craft is based on 45 degrees north latitude, the northern part of the United States. The upright triangle pattern is called the gnomon and it should have one right angle. Think of it as the hour hand on an analog clock, or a clock with hands.

MATERIALS
- Paper copy of sundial patterns (next page)
- 4 thumbtacks
- Wooden board or thick cardboard at least 6 inches square
- Scissors
- Craft knife
- Thin cardboard
- Tape
- Compass

DIRECTIONS
1. Make a copy of the patterns on the next page.
2. The pattern with the numbers is your sundial base. Cut at the 12:00 line. Tack the sundial base to the board.
3. Cut out the triangle. The bottom side of the triangle will have one right angle on the bottom, and the other angle will be the same as your latitude.

Gnomon

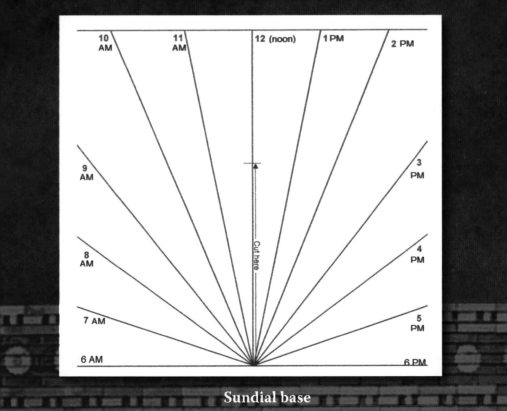

| 10 AM | 11 AM | 12 (noon) | 1 PM | 2 PM |

9 AM

8 AM

7 AM

Cut here

6 AM

3 PM

4 PM

5 PM

6 PM

Sundial base

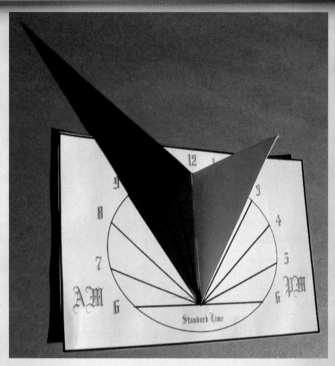

4. Either trace or glue the triangle on the piece of thin cardboard. Cut out the cardboard triangle.
5. Fold along the line at the bottom on the triangle. Slide the folded area under the cut in the sundial base. Be sure the long side of the triangle faces 12:00.
6. Use tape as needed to keep the gnomon standing up.
7. Using a compass, find magnetic north. Because magnetic north is not true north, use http://www.ngdc.noaa.gov/geomag-web/#declination to determine true north.
8. Set the sundial down on the ground with the arrow pointing north.
9. When the sun shines on your sundial, the shadow on the sundial should show the approximate time. For instance, if a shadow ends at 9 a.m., it should be around 9 a.m.

Babylonian Recipe: Barley Bread

Bread can be made from any type of grain, including wheat, corn, and barley. This flat bread is airy in the middle and crunchy around the edges.

INGREDIENTS

2   cups barley flour
2   teaspoons baking powder
1   teaspoon salt
¾   cup water
2   tablespoons olive oil
1   tablespoon flaxseed (linseed)
2   tablespoons sunflower seeds

INSTRUCTIONS

1. Preheat oven to 400°F. Lightly grease a baking sheet with cooking spray, butter, or oil.
2. Sift the barley flour, baking powder, and salt in a mixing bowl.
3. Blend the water, olive oil, flaxseed, and sunflower seeds in a blender or food processor until it becomes a liquid. Fold this liquid into the flour. Mix well with a spoon until it forms a dough.
4. Lay the dough onto a lightly floured surface. Using your hands, shape the dough into a flat circle about half an inch thick.
5. Slide the dough onto the baking sheet. Use a knife to make lines in the top of the loaf. With a fork, poke small holes all over the top of the bread.
6. Bake about 15 to 20 minutes. The bread should be pale gold when it's done. Cut the bread or break it into wedges along the lines. Serve warm.

BCE

4000	The civilization of Sumer begins.
2300	Babylon is mentioned for the first time; it begins as a small farming village.
1900	*The Epic of Gilgamesh* is written.
1894	The First Dynasty of Babylon begins as Sumu-Abum becomes the first ruler of a newly powerful Babylon.
1800	Babylonians use advanced mathematics, including algebra and square roots. They also begin to measure time.
1792	Hammurabi becomes the sixth king of the first Babylonian dynasty. He creates the Code of Hammurabi, most likely after 1762.
1750	Hammurabi dies.
1700	Babylonians invent the windmill to use for irrigation.
1600	Kassites begin ruling Babylon.
1225	The Assyrians conquer Babylon.
1168	The Elamites capture Babylon.
729	The Assyrians again conquer Babylon.
626	Nabopolassar conquers Assyria and becomes king of Babylon, starting the Neo-Babylonian dynasty, also known as the Chaldean empire.
605	Nebuchadnezzar II becomes king of Babylon, which grows into the most powerful city in the world.
587	Nebuchadnezzar II captures Jerusalem. He sends the people to Babylon to serve as slaves.

580	Cyrus the Great is born; he becomes Persian ruler about 550 and conquers countries throughout the Middle East.
539	Babylon is captured by Cyrus the Great and becomes part of the Persian Empire.
335–331	Alexander the Great defeats the Persians; he captures Babylon in 331.
323	Alexander the Great dies in Babylon.
CE	
640	Babylon becomes part of the Islamic empire.
1258	Mongol invaders destroy Baghdad.
1879	The Cyrus Cylinder is discovered; it describes the fall of Babylon.
1920	The modern country of Iraq is founded under British control.
1932	Iraq declares independence from Britain; it is ruled by King Faisal.
1958	Iraq becomes a republic.
1979–2003	Saddam Hussein, the fifth president of Iraq, contributes to the destruction of Babylonian artifacts.
2003	War in Iraq begins when the United States and Great Britain invade Iraq and remove Saddam Hussein from power.
2005	A new constitution is ratified in Iraq, establishing democracy there. The first democratic elections are held in January.
2006	Saddam Hussein is executed in Iraq for crimes committed during his rule.
2011	U.S. troops withdraw from Iraq.

Chapter 1: Babylon: A Wonder of the Ancient World

1. Joan Oates, *Babylon* (London: Thames & Hudson, 1979), p. 112.
2. Livius: Ancient Mesopotamia—Ziggurat http://www.livius.org/za-zn/ziggurat/ziggurat.html
3. Livius: Etemenanki (The Tower of Babel) http://www.livius.org/es-ez/etemenanki/etemenanki.html
4. Livius: Ancient Mesopotamia—Esagila http://www.livius.org/es-ez/esagila/esagila.html

Chapter 3: Gods and Kings

1. Think Quest Library: Seven Wonders of the Ancient World, Hanging Gardens of Babylon. http://library.thinkquest.org/C0123829/
2. Paul Brians, et al., *The Code of Hammurabi* [18th Century BCE], Washington State University, 1998. http://public.wsu.edu/~wldciv/world_civ_reader/world_civ_reader_1/Hammarabi.html

Chapter 4: The Fall of Babylon

1. Irving Finkel, Translation of the Text on the Cyrus Cylinder, The British Museum, http://www.britishmuseum.org/explore/highlights/article_index/c/cyrus_cylinder_-_translation.aspx
2. Ibid.
3. Ibid.

Chapter 5: Today's Babylon

1. Neil MacFarquhar, "Hussein's Babylon: A Beloved Atrocity," *The New York Times,* August 19, 2003. http://www.nytimes.com/2003/08/19/world/hussein-s-babylon-a-beloved-atrocity.html?n=Top%2fReference%2fTimes%20Topics%2fSubjects%2fT%2fTerrorism
2. World Monuments Fund: The Future of Babylon http://www.wmf.org/project/future-babylon

Works Consulted

Bauer, S. Wise. *The History of the Ancient World: From the Earliest Accounts to the Fall of Rome.* New York: W.W. Norton, 2007.

Brown, Dale. Mesopotamia: *The Mighty Kings.* Alexandria, Virginia: Time-Life Books, 1995.

Carey, John. *Eyewitness to History.* Cambridge: Massachusetts: Harvard University Press, 1987.

Fara, Patricia. *Science: A Four Thousand Year History.* New York: Oxford University Press, 2009.

Howe, John. *Lost Worlds.* New York: Kingfisher, 2009.

MacFarquhar, Neil. "Hussein's Babylon: A Beloved Atrocity." *The New York Times,* August 19, 2003.

Oates, Joan. *Babylon.* London: Thames & Hudson, 1979.

Books

Bendick, Jeanne. *Herodotus and the Road to History.* Bathgate, North Dakota: Bethlehem Books, 2009.

Davenport, John. *A Brief Political and Geographic History of the Middle East: Where Are Persia, Babylon, and the Ottoman Empire?* Hockessin, Delaware: Mitchell Lane Publishers, 2007.

Rustad, Martha E.H. *The Babylonians: Life in Ancient Babylon.* Minneapolis: Millbrook Press, 2010.

Scholl, Elizabeth J. *How'd They Do That ? Ancient Mesopotamia.* Hockessin, Delaware: Mitchell Lane Publishers, 2009.

Woods, Michael and Mary B. Woods. *Seven Wonders of the Ancient World.* Minneapolis: Twenty-First Century Books, 2009.

On the Internet

Assyrian International News Agency: Everyday Life in
	Babylon & Syria
	http://www.aina.org/books/eliba/eliba.htm

Babylonian and Akkadian Names
	http://www.peiraeuspubliclibrary.com/names/asia/
	babylonia.html

The British Museum: Explore World Cultures—Babylonians
	http://www.britishmuseum.org/explore/cultures/middle_
	east/babylonians.aspx

The British Museum: Mesopotamia
	http://www.mesopotamia.co.uk/

History World International: Babylonia
	http://history-world.org/babylonia.htm

Kidipede: Neo-Babylonians
	http://www.historyforkids.org/learn/westasia/history/baby
	lonians.htm

KidsGen: Seven Wonders of the World
	http://www.kidsgen.com/wonders_of_the_world/index.
	htm

Livius: Mesopotamia
	http://www.livius.org/babylonia.html

Pergamon Museum: Babylon Myth and Truth
	http://www.smb.museum/smb/babylon/show_text.
	php?lang=en

YouTube: British Museum Babylon Tower of Babel
	http://www.youtube.com/watch?v=t07tqOahDFU&feature
	=related

altar (AWL-tur)—A large table used for prayer.

archaeologist (ar-kee-AWL-uh-jist)—A person who studies past civilizations.

artifact (AR-tih-fakt)—An object made or used by humans in the past.

assassination (uh-sass-uh-NAY-shun)—The murder of a powerful person.

cuneiform (kyoo-NEE-uh-form)—Wedge-shaped writing used in ancient cultures.

debris (duh-BREE)—Pieces of something destroyed or broken.

declaration (deh-kluh-RAY-shun)—A formal announcement.

decree (deh-KREE)—An official decision.

dowry (DOW-ree)—The money or property a woman brings to a marriage.

dynasty (DY-nuh-stee)—A series of rulers related in some way.

epic (EH-pik)—A long story or poem that usually tells of heroes and battles.

excavate (EK-skuh-vayt)—To dig into the ground to find things from the past.

fertile (FUR-tuhl)—Good for growing crops.

frankincense (FRANG-kin-sens)—A sweet-smelling gum burned as incense.

horoscopes (HORE-oh-scopez)—Diagram of the heavens to predict births and important events in a person's life.

irrigate (EER-ih-gayt)—To supply water to crops.

legislation (leh-juhs-LAY-shun)—The creation of laws.

looting (LOO-ting)—Stealing during war or riots.

mausoleum (mah-zuh-LEE-um)—Named after the Tomb of Mausolus, a building in which people who have died are laid to rest.

pomegranate (PAH-muh-gran-uht)—A round reddish yellow fruit with red flesh and dozens of seeds surrounded by juice.

preamble (PREE-am-buhl)—An introductory statement.

scribe (SKRIBE)—A person who copies books, letters, and documents by hand.

sediment (SEH-duh-munt)—Rocks, sand, and dirt that settle in the bottom of liquid, such as a river.

shrine (SHRYN)—A holy or important place.

staple (STAY-pul)—A main type of food for a culture.

stylus (STY-lus)—A pointed tool for writing or cutting grooves into clay or stone.

teakwood (TEEK-wood)—Strong heavy wood from a tree in Asia.

trench (TRENCH)—A long narrow ditch, commonly used to protect soldiers during battle.

ventilation (ven-tuh-LAY-shun)—The process of letting fresh air in and stale air out.

water table (WAH-ter TAY-bul)—The level below which ground is soaked in water.

6-13